YOUR KNOWLEDGE HAS

- We will publish your bachelor's and master's thesis, essays and papers

- Your own eBook and book - sold worldwide in all relevant shops

- Earn money with each sale

Upload your text at www.GRIN.com
and publish for free

Strategic Management Audit Report for Amazon (2020)

Khaled Bekhet

Bibliographic information published by the German National Library:

The German National Library lists this publication in the National Bibliography; detailed bibliographic data are available on the Internet at http://dnb.dnb.de.

ISBN: 9783346651044
This book is also available as an ebook.

© GRIN Publishing GmbH
Nymphenburger Straße 86
80636 München

Print and binding: Books on Demand GmbH, Norderstedt, Germany
Printed on acid-free paper from responsible sources.

The present work has been carefully prepared. Nevertheless, authors and publishers do not incur liability for the correctness of information, notes, links and advice as well as any printing errors.

GRIN web shop: https://www.grin.com/document/1183677

Strategic Audit Report for Amazon

Table of Contents

Executive Summary

The purpose of this research is to examine Amazon's worldwide position, as well as how its present business plan compares to its rivals and fits within the company's global outlook. The research was done utilizing financial data and public information from the company's website to see where they shine and where they fall short.

To better analyze Amazon.com and identify areas for development, graphs and comparative studies were created. The charts and tables that support the data are included in the following report. According to the findings of the data analysis, Amazon is a very successful company that continues to be a dominant competitor in the online retail market.

The researcher applied the most known tools in strategic management to assess the company's competitive strategy,

The Company

Amazon started its activity in the market in July 1995 as an online book seller, within a month, the fledgling retailer had dispatched books to 45 countries and all 50 states in the United States. "Get large fast," as founder Jeff Bezos put it, and Seattle-based Amazon grew into an e-commerce behemoth, offering everything from groceries to furniture to live ladybugs, and revolutionizing the way people buy.

After graduating from Princeton University with a bachelor's degree in computer science and electrical engineering in 1986, Bezos worked in the financial services business in New York City. He relocated to Washington state in 1994 after discovering the financial potential of the

Internet and believing that books may sell well online. After the word Cadabra (as in abracadabra) was misheard as "cadaver," Bezos decided to rename his company Amazon, after the massive river in South America, a nickname he felt would not limit him to selling only one sort of goods or service.

Bezos allowed a small number of friends and former coworkers to try out a test version of Amazon's website in the spring of 1995, and the first-ever order for a scientific book titled Fluid Concepts and Creative Analogies was placed on April 3 of that year. When Amazon.com first went up to the general public in July 1995, the firm boldly marketed itself as "Earth's biggest bookshop," despite the fact that sales were first fueled largely by word of mouth, and Bezos assisted with order assembly and delivery to the post office.

Amazon had generated $15.7 million in sales by the end of 1996, and Bezos took the firm public in 1997 with an IPO that garnered $54 million. Bezos personally delivered the one-millionth order to a client in Japan who had ordered a Windows NT handbook and a Princess Diana biography the same year. Amazon began selling music CDs in 1998, and by the following year, it had expanded into other product categories such as toys, electronics, and tools.

Amazon had shipped 20 million goods to 150 countries across the world by December 1999. Bezos was selected Person of the Year by Time magazine in the same month. In the year 2000, Amazon launched a service that allowed individual sellers and other third-party merchants to offer their goods alongside Amazon's own. Meanwhile, Amazon continued to invest extensively in expansion, and it didn't turn a profit for the first time until 2003.

Amazon introduced the Kindle e-reader in 2007, and four years later, the business declared that e-books were outselling print books. The Kindle Fire, Amazon's tablet computer, was also introduced in 2011. Amazon introduced cloud computing and video on demand services in 2006, a film and television series development studio in 2010, and an online fine art marketplace in 2013, which has exhibited original works by artists such as Claude Monet and Norman Rockwell. Additionally, Amazon has purchased several businesses, including Zappos and Whole Foods. Amazon overtook Walmart as the world's most valuable retailer in 2015. Amazon's market worth was $250 billion two decades after its foundation, with Bezos still at the helm. Bezos was ranked the world's richest man in 2017. The growing popularity of the online retail business is a result of governmental encouragement. However, this growing industry of online retailing can also prove to be a risk for Amazon facing tough competition from big brands, especially foreign companies making their way into online retail. In 2017, Bezos was named the richest man in the world. In July 5, 2021, Bezos stepped down as CEO of Amazon to focus on his aerospace company Blue Origin. [1i]

---

[1] https://www.history.com/this-day-in-history/amazon-opens-for-business

In 2021, Amazon acquired Souq.com in Egypt, to start a new phase with new market.

Anmerkung der Redaktion: Diese Abbildung wurde aus urheberrechtlichen Gründen entfernt.

Amazon's mission statement:

"We strive to offer our customers the lowest possible prices, the best available selection, and the utmost convenience" [2ii]

This company objective guarantees appealing e-commerce services to meet the expectations of target clients. Price, selection, and convenience are all factors that the firm considers. In this context, Amazon's corporate mission statement identifies the following characteristics:

- Lowest Price
- Best selection

---

[2] http://panmore.com/amazon-com-inc-vision-statement-mission-statement-analysis

- Utmost convenience

The pricing methods contained in Amazon.com Inc.'s marketing mix, or 4P, are guided by the mission statement's "lowest prices" component. The company's e-commerce website and services are appealing because of their low rates. A related strategic goal is to reduce operating expenses so that the company may lower pricing. The finest selection is also included in Amazon's company goal statement. Customers are drawn to the company's website because of the large number of items available. Furthermore, Amazon.com Inc.'s business objective promotes convenience, such as using the Internet to access the company's items. Consumers' usage of "convenience" as a factor when evaluating the quality and attractiveness of online retail services has prompted this trait.

Amazon's corporate vision statement:

Amazon's corporate vision is *"to be Earth's most customer-centric company, where customers can find and discover anything they might want to buy online"* [3]

The major goal of the business organization is to become the top e-commerce firm in the world, as stated in this vision statement. In this sense, Amazon's corporate vision statement identifies the following characteristics:

- Global reach

- Customer-Centric approach

- Widest selection of products

---

[3] http://panmore.com/amazon-com-inc-vision-statement-mission-statement-analysis

Amazon.com Inc.'s vision statement's "global reach" component is all about worldwide supremacy in the e-commerce business. For example, mentioning "Earth" as the market indicates that the firm intends to continue developing internationally. As a result, a strategic goal of Amazon.com Inc.'s general strategy and intense growth plans is worldwide expansion, particularly through market penetration and market development. The customer-centric strategy outlined in Amazon's corporate vision statement demonstrates that customers are one of the most significant stakeholders in the online retail industry. This point of view is consistent with Amazon.com Inc.'s corporate social responsibility policy for its stakeholders. Furthermore, the corporate strategy shows that efforts to widen the product mix would continue. These initiatives contribute to the company's growth and make its services more appealing to target customers.[iii]

Amazon's Generic Strategy (Porter's Model)

Amazon's generic competitive advantage approach is cost leadership. The goal of this general competitive strategy is to reduce operating expenses as much as possible. Amazon.com, for example, leverages modern processing and networking technology to maximize operational efficiency, resulting in lower costs. Process automation, which is commonly utilized in purchase processing, scheduling, and other operational procedures, is beneficial to the organization given the nature of e-commerce. Amazon.com Inc. can reduce the cost of its online shopping and other services because to these advantages.

Building e-commerce competitive advantage through continual enhancement of information technology infrastructure is a strategic aim tied to Amazon's cost leadership general strategy. In this regard, the corporation has set a strategic goal to invest extensively in research and development (R&D) in order to improve the performance of its IT resources. Furthermore,

Amazon.com Inc. is pushed to lower its prices by its generic competitive strategy of cost leadership. Amazon's marketing mix is influenced by this strategic goal. The inexpensive costs play a big role in recruiting customers. As a result of the general strategy of cost leadership, Amazon.com Inc. gains a competitive advantage to support the fulfilment of its mission and vision statements, particularly in terms of online retail worldwide expansion and leadership.

Products and Services

Amazon currently owns 91 different private label brands that they sell on their platform.

- Amazon.com
- Amazon Marketplace
- Amazon Pantry
- Amazon Fresh
- Amazon Payments
- Amazon Games
- Amazon Art
- Amazon Video
- Amazon Basics
- Amazon Elements
- Amazon Kindle Fire
- Amazon Prime Air
- Amazon Go
- Amazon Music Unlimited
- Amazon Tickets
- Amazon Web Services
- Amazon Prime
- Amazon Music
- Amazon Fire Tv
- Echo and Alexa
- Audible

External Environment

PESTEL Analysis [4][iv]

Introduction:

PESTEL Analysis is a well-thought-out plan for business growth and expansion. This framework, similar to SWOT analysis, gives firms a broad perspective of their strengths and weaknesses by examining many elements that influence the organization's performance.

Companies need such tactics to comprehend their current status and operation, as well as to enhance their offerings and performance. It takes into account the macro, distant environment and offers the dangers and possibilities to the businesses who are monitoring the many elements. From six viewpoints, this Amazon PESTEL research provides extensive explanations of why Amazon can stand out in such severe rivals.

---

[4] https://www.edrawmax.com/article/amazon-pestel-analysis.html

Political Factors

The growth of an organization in any particular state or country is determined by the government, its policies, and its rules. All of these components are political factors in a PESTEL study, and they include tax rules and regulations, corruption, international trade policy, and labor legislation.

- It investigates government intervention and the potential for the industry to thrive in that location.
- Governmental assistance for cybersecurity and seamless e-commerce operations benefits Amazon's company. Furthermore, Amazon benefits from the political stability of wealthy countries.
- Government support has contributed to the rise in popularity of internet retailing. However, Amazon may face stiff competition from huge brands, particularly international corporations looking to enter the online retail market, as the online retailing sector grows. The growing popularity of the online retail business is a result of governmental encouragement. However, this growing industry of online retailing can also prove to be a risk for Amazon facing tough competition from big brands, especially foreign companies making their way into online retail.

Ecological Factors

Pollution and climate change have heightened public awareness of environmental issues. The ecological factor assesses whether the firm has a high probability of surviving in light of its environmental sensitivity. Companies that focus on environmentally friendly products and services, use renewable energy, and consider a long-term future gain an advantage.

- Amazon has development potential, according to PESTEL analysis, when considering its ecological element. Its growing interest in environmental initiatives, company sustainability, and low-carbon lifestyle and waste management measures may help it expand its market.

Social Factors

Knowledge customer behavior leads to a better understanding of product demand and supply. It is mostly dictated by a location's sociocultural heritage. Companies can analyze the prospective market by considering social aspects such as cultural shift, education level, and population.

- Amazon relies on technology to replace employees. In terms of societal considerations, the pace of declining work chances might be a danger to the organization.
- On the other side, the corporation will gain from the expanding trend of online buying and greater consumerism. Amazon's appeal among young and elderly individuals who don't want to leave their homes specially during the COVID 19 pandemic, is due to its easy availability of items and doorstep delivery.

Technological Factors

Another important component in identifying a company's strengths and weaknesses is technological innovation. Automation, technological innovation, change, and technical understanding are all variables that assist businesses in making informed decisions about their future. It assists them in implementing new technologies, as well as planning manufacturing, logistics, and distribution.

- Amazon's growth of activities has brought them into conflict with technological companies. Amazon's ability to reach out to customers in novel and creative ways is unrivalled. They are constantly looking for innovative and more efficient ways to transport and deliver items.
- They are easily accessible via the live chat option. As a result, Amazon intends to expand its workforce in order to progress technologically. It will assist them in providing an improved client experience.

Economic Factors:

The revenue of a corporation is influenced by economic variables. Unemployment rates, borrowing rates, raw material costs, and other factors are all taken into consideration. This component informs the organization about the purchasing power of its customers, allowing it to adjust its pricing, products, and services accordingly. It has a direct impact on the profitability of a firm.

- Despite the fact that Amazon has expanded its services globally with official assistance, taxes remain a continual barrier, especially in Asian nations, with their ever-changing numbers.
- Even when customers are not looking for anything pricey, Amazon's wide selection appeals to them. Economic stability in emerging nations provides Amazon with expansion chances.

Legal Factors

Rules and regulations are addressed by legal considerations, which are comparable to political factors. Organizations must follow laws governing industry regulation, employee health and safety, consumer legislation, and more in order to have a full understanding of the dos and don'ts of operating in a certain region.

- Amazon adheres to the rules and regulations while growing its wings globally. It is focused on cybersecurity, with customer protection as a priority.
- It has strengthened its brand image through efforts such as complicated environmental protection rules. Changes in import and export policies, on the other hand, will make it easier for the company to face competition.

Summary

Competitive environment [5v]
(Porter Five Forces Model)

Competitive Rivalry > High

This is because the number of the competitors in the recent years has grown. Also, traditional brands are offering online sales giving further competition to these online retailers.

Threats of New Entrants > Low

- It's not easy for a new entrant to compete in the same level, it would take a lot of investment, resources.
- To compete with the largest online store, new entrants would have to offer massive quantities of inventory, competitive pricing, and timely delivery.

Bargaining Power of Suppliers > Low

- Because Amazon has so many suppliers, the suppliers have little negotiation leverage.
- Amazon has a large number of suppliers, who must adhere to Amazon's standards.
- Since Amazon is such a massive buying platform, suppliers would not try to undercut them.
- Suppliers can't usually raise input prices since Amazon will move on to the next one.

---

[5] https://www.porteranalysis.com/porters-five-forces-analysis-of-amazon/

Bargaining Power of Buyers > High

- Customer satisfaction and product quality are very important to Amazon. It guarantees that items are delivered on schedule, and that any returns or replacements are handled efficiently in order to transform first-time consumers into repeat customers.
- Switching cost of the buyers is low.
- Buyers are well-informed, and because to the growing popularity of internet commerce, they have a variety of alternatives.

Threats of Substitutes > High

- Amazon caters to customer requirements, but numerous enterprises may provide goods equivalents.
- Alternatives to Amazon include Walmart, branded storefronts, and online sites for brands that Amazon also offers.
- A single unpleasant encounter with an online merchant is enough to turn a buyer away.

IFE Analysis

Amazon's IFE shows the company's strengths and weaknesses that we believe are the most important. Amazon's top three strengths were strong brand name, customer loyalty and the high-quality management team. We also discovered that the company's top problems were margin shrinking and employee moral. The top strengths and weaknesses we discovered are depicted in the IFE Matrix below.

	Strengths	Weight	Rating	Weighted Score
1	Strong brand name	0.10	4	0.40
2	Low cost structure	0.05	3	0.15
3	High quality management team	0.10	4	0.40
4	Customer Loyalty	0.10	4	0.40
5	Effective post sales services	0.05	3	0.15
6	Developed and upgraded technology: Software and Hardware	0.08	3	0.24
7	Great Suply Chain	0.05	4	0.20
8	Diversification	0.05	3	0.15
9	Market Leader	0.08	4	0.32
10	Logistics and distrubution system	0.07	3	0.21

	Weaknesses	Weight	Rating	Weighted Score
1	Product quality from international sellers (China)	0.03	2	0.06
2	Workplace conditions	0.02	2	0.04
3	Margin shrinking due to free shipping and operaing in near zero	0.04	2	0.08
4	Anti-Trust Charges in the Europian Union	0.02	1	0.02
5	Diversification	0.03	1	0.03
6	Employee Moral, specially warehouse workers	0.04	2	0.08
7	Seller Relationship	0.04	1	0.04
8	Easily replicable business concept	0.02	1	0.02
9	Declining Customer Safety	0.02	2	0.04
10	Unfair use of Third-Party Data	0.01	1	0.01
	Total IFE Score	**1.00**		**3.04**

EFE Analysis

Amazon's EFE outlines the company's Opportunity and Threats. The top two opportunities for Amazon were Growth of Internet users; predominantly in international markets and E-commerce expansion in Asia and the Pacific. A cyber security breach and a competitor replicating their business model were both identified as two of the company's top threats. The top opportunities and threats we found are depicted in the EFE Matrix below.

	Opportunities	Weight	Rating	Weighted Score
1	Increasing the number of buyers over the Internet	0.06	3	0.18
2	Positive changes in book selling business and market	0.06	4	0.24
3	Growth of Internet users; predominantly in international markets	0.10	3	0.3
4	E-commerce expansion in Asia and the Pacific	0.07	2	0.14
5	Increasing product categories	0.06	4	0.24
6	24% expected increase in online retail sales in 2025	0.05	3	0.15
7	Young people's desire of new technology and innovative ideas	0.03	4	0.12
8	Weak Dollar will help the value of International currency	0.03	2	0.06
9	Self-Driving Technology	0.04	3	0.12
10	0	0.00	0	0

	Threats	Weight	Rating	Weighted Score
1	eBay, Barnes & Nobles, OLX and Book-A-Million,	0.15	3	0.45
2	Possible rejection to on-line sales in international markets due to introduction of new taxes	0.03	3	0.09
3	Competition in the global market	0.04	3	0.12
4	Seasonal products create shifting revenues	0.03	2	0.06
5	Competition from the local market	0.04	2	0.08
6	Cybersecurity Breach	0.10	4	0.40
7	Political contraits between USA and other Countries	0.03	2	0.06
8	Lawsuits from Copetitors	0.03	3	0.09
9	Counterfeits Goods	0.05	2	0.10
10	0	0.00	0	0.00
	Total EFE Score	1.00		3.00

CPM Matrix

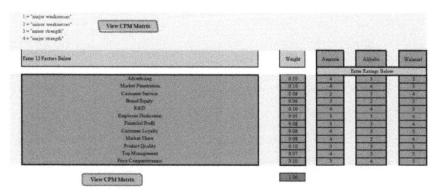

Critical Success Factors	Weight	Amazon		Alibaba		Walmart	
		Rating	**Score**	**Rating**	**Score**	**Rating**	**Score**
Advertising	0.10	4	0.40	3	0.30	3	0.30
Market Penetration	0.10	4	0.40	4	0.40	3	0.30
Customer Service	0.08	3	0.24	3	0.24	4	0.32
Brand Equity	0.06	3	0.18	2	0.12	3	0.18
R&D	0.10	4	0.40	4	0.40	3	0.30
Employee Dedication	0.05	3	0.15	3	0.15	4	0.20
Financial Profit	0.08	3	0.24	3	0.24	4	0.32
Customer Loyalty	0.08	4	0.32	3	0.24	3	0.24
Market Share	0.08	4	0.32	2	0.16	4	0.32
Product Quality	0.10	3	0.30	3	0.30	3	0.30
Top Management	0.07	4	0.28	3	0.21	3	0.21
Price Competitiveness	0.10	3	0.30	4	0.40	3	0.30
Totals	**1.00**		**3.53**		**3.16**		**3.29**

IE Matrix

Based on the IFE and EFE data, we came up with the below IE matrix which reflect the very strong position of Amazon in the market and locate at the "Grow and Build" quadrant.

Accordingly, the suggested strategy for Amazon can be summarized in the following:

- Backward, Forward or Horizontal Integration
- Market Penetration
- Market Development
- Product Development

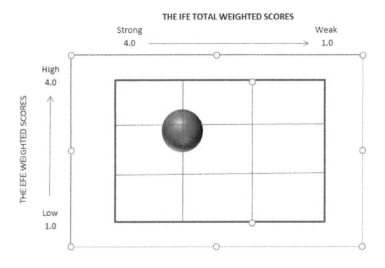

VRIO Framework [6][vi]

- Competitive Advantages, Core Competencies:

Amazon.com Inc. is an e-commerce company that started out specializing in online retail but has subsequently evolved to include a variety of online and offline services. A VRIO analysis of Amazon explains how the company grows and maintains its market position. The VRIO model is based on Jay B. Barney's internal analysis approach for determining a firm's competitive advantages. The competitive advantages of Amazon.com are built on a number of resources and business competencies. Nonetheless, Amazon's information technology assets, as well as associated resources and competencies, remain at its heart. The VRIO analytical model assists the company's decision-makers in developing optimum strategic plans and strategic objectives in order to compete against Walmart, Costco, Target, Macy's, and Nordstrom. Amazon profits from its core capabilities, but it has to build new core skills and reinforce current ones to avoid interruptions in its worldwide business's development.

VRIO Analysis Table – Amazon.com Inc.

The core competencies of Amazon are built on organizational skills and business resources that meet all of the VRIO requirements (value, rarity, inimitability, and organization). Many of the firm's resources and skills meet only one or a few of these requirements, yet they nonetheless help the organization flourish. Amazon's non-core and core competences are summarized in the VRIO table below:

---

[6] https://www.rancord.org/amazon-vrio-analysis-competitive-advantages-core-competencies

Amazon's Organizational Resources & Capabilities	V	R	I	O
Increased presence in the physical world	✔			
Online services are becoming increasingly diverse.	✔			
Private label products increasing portfolio	✔			
A vast distribution network that includes domestic, regional, and international collaborations	✔	✔		
Expertise based on years of e-commerce experience	✔	✔		
Warehouses and delivery hubs in strategic locations	✔	✔		
Sustained Competitive Advantage(s):				
High brand equity on a global scale	✔	✔	✔	✔
High market capitalization	✔	✔	✔	✔
Affiliates from throughout the world help to broaden the reach of the company's global market.	✔	✔	✔	✔
Artificial intelligence capabilities	✔	✔	✔	✔

- Non-core Competencies:

Amazon.com's non-core capabilities, as seen in the VRIO table above, include the company's developing brick-and-mortar presence. This expertise is significant and contributes to competitive advantage, but it is also replicable and not uncommon, given that big corporations such as Walmart have substantial physical presences. Also, Amazon's expanding range of online services is beneficial in terms of diversifying revenue streams, but it is neither unique or unique because other digital companies provide similar services. Furthermore, the VRIO table demonstrates that the company's expanding array of private label items diversifies its offers, expands market presence, and raises earnings. Amazon Basics, for example, is a private label that allows the corporation to compete directly with other online and non-online vendors.

Although private labelling is beneficial to the business, it is neither unusual nor unique. Private labelling may be implemented by even small firms.

Value Chain Analysis [vii]

Primary Activities

Important: The primary activities' purpose is to add value to the firm that surpasses the cost of operation, resulting in increased profit.

Primary activities in the Amazon value chain are those that form the foundation of the company model by supplying consumers with the services they demand. To obtain a competitive edge, these activities include the acquisition of raw materials and products, operations to convert the procured resources to finished goods, and finally high-quality services, sales, and marketing. The five main actions are described in full below.

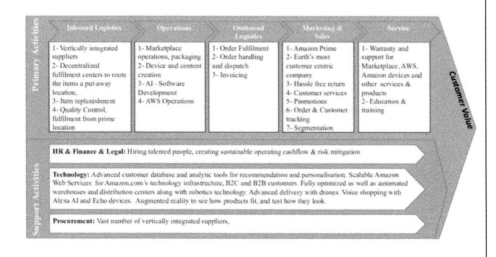

	Inbound Logistics	Operations	Outbound Logistics	Marketing & Sales	Service
Primary Activities	1- Vertically integrated suppliers 2- Decentralized fulfilment centers to route the items a put-away location, 3- Item replenishment 4- Quality Control, fulfilment from prime location	1- Marketplace operations, packaging 2- Device and content creation 3- AI - Software Development 4- AWS Operations	1- Order Fulfilment 2- Order handling and dispatch 3- Invoicing	1- Amazon Prime 2- Earth's most customer centric company 3- Hassle free return 4- Customer services 5- Promotions 6- Order & Customer tracking 7- Segmentation	1- Warranty and support for Marketplace, AWS, Amazon devices and other services & products 2- Education & training

HR & Finance & Legal: Hiring talented people, creating sustainable operating cashflow & risk mitigation

Technology: Advanced customer database and analytic tools for recommendation and personalisation. Scalable Amazon Web Services for Amazon.com's technology infrastructure, B2C and B2B customers. Fully optimized as well as automated warehouses and distribution centers along with robotics technology. Advanced delivery with drones. Voice shopping with Alexa AI and Echo devices. Augmented reality to see how products fit, and test how they look.

Procurement: Vast number of vertically integrated suppliers,

- Inbound Logistics

The term "inbound logistics" refers to the process of procuring raw materials. However, because Amazon does not often make its own items, its Fulfillment by Amazon service is its inbound logistics, which it supplies to sellers. Because of its logistics and the efficiency of its delivery and returns, Amazon stands apart in the market. It offers dependable services and is in charge of logistics, customer care, and product returns. At the same time, for Amazon value chain analysis, effective logistics infrastructure includes incoming logistics.

- Operations

Operations are actions that turn raw resources into finished items in a value chain analysis. Amazon has a variety of channels that it covers with its activities. These categories are divided by geography, with the North American section and the international segment being the most prominent. The Amazon Web Services division is the third (AWS). Computing, storage, cloud infrastructure, databases, and other services are all part of AWS. Amazon gains a competitive edge from these businesses in terms of services and operations.

Amazon's profile is enhanced through innovative and reliable solutions. Cloud storage, AWS, and cloud computing all began as internal corporate solutions. However, when Amazon marketed these solutions, their sophistication and resilience provided them with a new revenue stream. As a result, the activities give the firm a competitive edge.

- Outbound Logistics

The storage, supply, and distribution of completed goods are all part of outbound logistics. The 175 fulfilment facilities throughout the world are important to Amazon's outbound logistics. Robotic technology is used to help Amazon's inventory fulfilment. Finished product storage, transportation, and distribution activities. Amazon's outbound logistics comprise a variety of processes. Fulfillment by Amazon is in charge of managing, storing, and shipping all orders. For effective outbound logistics, it involves shipping providers and Amazon's logistic infrastructure, which includes aircraft, ships, trucks, and drones.

Aside from that, outbound logistics also includes digital product distribution. It contains digital books, media, and other items. Then there's another outbound logistics route for physical stores.

- Marketing and Sales

Of course, this massive marketing and advertising effort is spread over several channels, media, and has a worldwide reach and influence. Print and media advertisements, sales promotions, events, public relations, and focused consumer marketing are all part of it. Aside from direct and popular marketing, Amazon uses a variety of different methods to draw people to its brand. It promotes itself as a preferred brand by offering low prices, quick delivery, and Amazon Prime services.

- Service

Value chain analysis of Amazon shows that the services provided by the organization play a vital role in acquiring a competitive advantage. It provides premium services for the end customers and the vendors that eventually result in a sleek and reliable business model for everyone. It provides full support, including training, literature, and support facilities for vendors. At the same time, the end customer can use Amazon Marketplace and prime services for more advantages. After-sale service is another great endeavor from Amazon.

Support Activities

Infrastructure, human resource management, and procurement are examples of secondary or support activities. Support activities offer a foundation for primary activities to function correctly and efficiently.

- Infrastructure

Amazon is a behemoth in the commercial world, and it would undoubtedly collapse if it didn't have a solid infrastructure to support it. Amazon has put money, time, and effort into developing a scalable and dependable business strategy to support its massive scale and market position. Offline structures such as shipping, hiring, and delivery are included. At the same time, the online assistance and digital solutions are second to none. The organization features a smooth customer service and employee management infrastructure in addition to its backend management.

- Human Resource Management

Without Amazon's HR management department, the value chain analysis cannot be completed. Amazon has a permanent staff, as well as in-house workers, overseas employees, contractors, and a contingent workforce. Amazon features a technologically enabled firm architecture that ensures optimum collaboration between the company and its employees. It has the most loyal staff and the lowest turnover because to its incentives program and acknowledgement of outstanding performance.

- Technology Development

Amazon has not only shown its physical product success, but it has also kept a close eye on the digital front. Processes and solutions such as cloud computing and cloud storage, which began as internal corporate processes to handle operations, have since become industry standards.

- Procurement

The company's procurement is handled via the sales and operations (S&OP) process. Forecasting and just-in-time inventory principles are used to manage inventory in this system.

Amazon's SWOT Matrix

	Internal Strengths S1- Strong brand name S2- Low cost structure S3- High quality management team S4- Customer Loyalty S5-Effective post sales services S6- Developed and upgraded technology: Software and Hardware S7- Great Supply Chain	**Internal Weaknesses** W1- Product quality from China W2- Margin shrinking due to free shipping and operating in near zero margin business models W3- Relying only on online retailing W4- Employee Moral, specially warehouse workers W5- Seller Relationship
External Opportunities O1- Increasing the number of buyers over the Internet O2- Growth of Internet users O3- E-commerce expansion in Asia and the Pacific O4- Increasing product categories O5- Young people's desire of new technology and innovative ideas O6- Self-Driving Technology	**SO Strategies** (S1 O1 O2) Market penetration, Market development. (S1 S4 O4) Increase diversification, Product development. (S6 O5 O6) Take advantage of high-tech strength to make more investment for more market penetration	**WO Strategies** (W4 O6) Maximize the use of technology to replace the human capital with machines to reduce the moral issues. (W5 O5 O6) Find a way to improve the sellers' relationship by taking the advantage of innovative ideas and self-driving technology (W3 O4) Establish physical stores for more product categories
External Threats T1- Competition in the global market T2- Seasonal products create shifting revenues T3- Competition from the local market T4- Counterfeits Goods	**ST Strategies** (S2 T1 T3) Use the low-cost structure to gain more market shares against global and local competitors. (S3 T4) High quality mgt team can control and eliminate the counterfeits goods (S4 T2) Use the customer loyalty strength to make high revenue in the low season	**WT Strategies** (W1 T1 T3) Avoid the low-quality products imported from China to reduce the high competency from other retailers.

SPACE Matrix

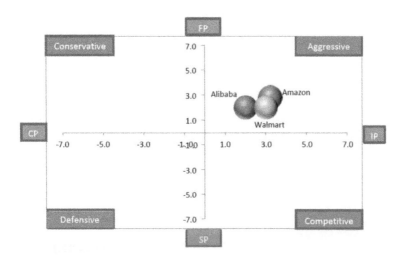

Internal Analysis:		External Analysis:	
Financial Position (FP)		**Stability Position (SP)**	
Revenue	6	Rate of Inflation	-2
Net Income	5	Technological Changes	-1
Inventory Turnover	5	Price Elasticity of Demand	-2
Debt to Equity	5	Competitive Pressure	-3
Current Ratio	5	Barriers to Entry into Market	-4
Financial Position (FP) Average	5.2	**Stability Position (SP) Average**	-2.4

Internal Analysis:		External Analysis:	
Competitive Position (CP)		**Industry Position (IP)**	
Market Share	-2	Growth Potential	6
Product Quality	-2	Financial Stability	5
Customer Loyalty	-1	Ease of Entry into Market	3
Technological know-how	-2	Resource Utilization	4
Control over Suppliers and Distributors	-1	Profit Potential	6
Competitive Position (CP) Average	-1.6	**Industry Position (IP) Average**	4.8

The space matrix places all three organizations in the aggressive category. On the x-axis, Amazon and Walmart are tied, while Alibaba is less than both. Amazon outperforms Alibaba and Walmart in terms of industry strength. Amazon leads on the y-axis due to their financial strength.

Alibaba has more financial strength than Amazon, but lacks the industry strength that Amazon possesses. Amazon outperforms Walmart in terms of financial and industry strength.

One suggestion is for Amazon to build more private brands, as the firm already has industry strength and releasing more of their own brands into the market will continue to improve the company's brand. Having more private brands, higher than Walmart's and Alibaba's private brand approach, would make Amazon a more leader corporation. Moving into the grocery industry is the second option, which would maximize their market share as well as product and market development. Amazon has a wide range of items, but competing in the grocery and delivery industries would expand their product line and market.

Strategy recommendations

Based on all the mentioned analysis and matrixes, there are some recommended strategies to be followed by Amazon according. Those strategies can be summarized in

1- Market penetration

2- Market Development

3- Backward or Forward and horizontal Integration

4- Product development

In the coming analysis, we are going to focus only on the Market Penetration and Market Development

QSPM Matrix

Based on the recommended strategies mentioned above, here is the QSPM matrix for both of them.

			Market Penetration		Market Development	
	Strengths	**Weight**	**AS**	**TAS**	**AS**	**TAS**
1	Strong brand name	0.10	3	0.30	4	0.40
2	Low cost structure	0.05	3	0.15	4	0.20
3	High quality management team	0.10	3	0.30	4	0.40
4	Customer Loyalty	0.10	3	0.30	4	0.40
5	Effective post sales services	0.05	2	0.10	4	0.20
6	Developed and upgraded technology: Software and Hardware	0.08	2	0.16	3	0.24
7	Great Supply Chain	0.05	4	0.20	3	0.15
8	Diversification	0.05	4	0.20	3	0.15
9	Market Leader	0.08	3	0.24	4	0.32
10	Logistics and distribution system	0.07	3	0.21	4	0.28

			Market Penetration		Market Development	
	Weaknesses	**Weight**	**AS**	**TAS**	**AS**	**TAS**
1	Product quality from international sellers (China)	0.03	1	0.03	2	0.06
2	Workplace conditions	0.02	2	0.04	3	0.06
3	Margin shrinking due to free shipping and operaing in near zero margin business models	0.04	0	0.00	2	0.08
4	Anti-Trust Charges in the Europian Union	0.02	2	0.04	0	0.00
5	Diversification	0.03	3	0.09	2	0.06
6	Employee Moral, specially warehouse workers	0.04	0	0.00	2	0.08
7	Seller Relationship	0.04	0	0.00	2	0.08
8	Easily replicable business concept	0.02	1	0.02	2	0.04
9	Declining Customer Safety	0.02	1	0.02	2	0.04
10	Unfair use of Third-Party Data	0.01	0	0.00	2	0.02

			Market Penetration		Market Development	
Opportunities	**Weight**	**AS**	**TAS**	**AS**	**TAS**
1	Increasing the number of buyers over the Internet	0.06	4	0.24	3	0.18
2	Positive changes in book selling business and market	0.06	1	0.06	2	0.12
3	Growth of Internet users; predominantly in international markets	0.10	3	0.30	1	0.10
4	E-commerce expansion in Asia and the Pacific	0.07	3	0.21	1	0.07
5	Increasing product categories	0.06	3	0.18	2	0.12
6	24% expected increase in online retail sales in 2025	0.05	2	0.10	3	0.15
7	Young people's desire of new technology and innovative ideas	0.03	3	0.09	2	0.06
8	Weak Dollar will help the value of International currency	0.03	3	0.09	2	0.06
9	Self-Driving Technology	0.04	2	0.08	3	0.12
10	0	0.00	0	0.00	0	0.00

			Market Penetration		Market Development	
Threats	**Weight**	**AS**	**TAS**	**AS**	**TAS**
1	Million,	0.15	2	0.30	3	0.45
2	Possible rejection to on-line sales in international markets due to introduction of new taxes	0.03	3	0.09	1	0.03
3	Competition in the global market	0.04	3	0.12	1	0.04
4	Seasonal products create shifting revenues	0.03	1	0.03	3	0.09
5	Competition from the local market	0.04	0	0.00	3	0.12
6	Cybersecurity Breach	0.10	1	0.10	2	0.20
7	Political contraits between USA and other Countries	0.03	0	0.00	1	0.03
8	Lawsuits from Copetitors	0.03	1	0.03	2	0.06
9	Counterfeits Goods	0.05	0	0.00	1	0.05
10	0	0.00	0	0.00	0	0.00
	STAS			**4.42**		**5.31**

Strategy Recommendations

Based on the above analysis that show the attractiveness of each strategy, we found that market development has a total attractiveness score of 5.31 while the market penetration has 4.42 which means that the most preferable strategy in the current situation is Market Development.

Exploring new markets to sell current items is what market development is all about. Over the years, Amazon has created a tremendous number of new marketplaces. Outside of the United States, its products are distributed to over 100 nations and territories (Delfino, 2020). Its primary markets are the United States (home market), the United Kingdom, Germany, and Japan (Coppola, 2021).

Amazon, on the other hand, failed in one of its most promising markets, China. It first arrived in the country in 2004 and quickly made a name for itself. However, it declared in 2019 that it will shut down its company due to competition from Alibaba and JD.com (Kharpal, 2019).

Existing products are sold into new markets as part of market development strategies. This strategy is a little riskier than market penetration. The following are some examples of varied focus regions:

- New area development programs
- New channels
- New packaging
- New pricing

The fundamental goal of this approach is to enter and develop in new markets. Amazon.com Inc. expands the number of countries where its services are available. Consumers in the United

States, for example, were the first to benefit from the company's online shopping offerings. Amazon currently has online stores in over ten countries, including Canada, the United Kingdom, China, and India. Each new country is viewed as a new market, providing potential for the company to expand. Amazon's generic approach creates a competitive advantage that allows the business to pursue this aggressive market expansion plan. Amazon.com has set a strategic goal as part of its aggressive expansion plan to launch new online retail websites in nations where the firm has expanded its worldwide market reach. [viii]

Aside to that, developing Amazon's proprietary brands and promoting them to the company's devoted consumer base. The strategic investment in selling their own branded items on the Amazon platform will contribute to Amazon's low-cost value. Through its accelerator program, Amazon has access to a large number of firms that they may buy and rebrand as their own. Amazon.com will make more money if it can offer more private brands on its platform and outsell other items.

Also, expand the grocery retailing by using existing business expertise to create a more effective grocery delivery service for Amazon consumers. Amazon now offers two grocery-based services: Amazon Fresh and Amazon Go. This would necessitate a greater physical presence.

Each Amazon Go store costs around a million dollars to build. There are now 21 Amazon Go convenience shops that enable "checkout list" shopping. Amazon has the potential to expand this service to most big and mid-sized cities in the United States, and then to the rest of the world. Amazon may use their Whole Foods acquisition to grow the brand and reach more people by offering grocery delivery through those locations.

References

Article Title: Amazon opens for business
[i] https://www.history.com/this-day-in-history/amazon-opens-for-business

Amazon.com's Corporate Mission & Vision Statement
[ii] http://panmore.com/amazon-com-inc-vision-statement-mission-statement-analysis
[iii] Amazon Web Services (AWS) – Cloud Computing Services.
Amazon.com Inc.'s E-commerce Website.
Amazon.com, Inc. – Form 10-K.
D'Urso, S. C. (2018). Towards the final frontier: Using strategic
[iv] Amazon PESTEL Analysis
https://www.edrawmax.com/article/amazon-pestel-analysis.html
[v] Porter five forces analysis of Amazon
https://www.porteranalysis.com/porters-five-forces-analysis-of-amazon/

[vi] Amazon VRIO Analysis – Competitive Advantages, Core Competencies
https://www.rancord.org/amazon-vrio-analysis-competitive-advantages-core-competencies

[vii] John D., 2020. 'Amazon Value Chain Analysis', BUSINESS RESEARCH METHODOLOGY, [online]. Available at:
https://research-methodology.net/amazon-value-chain-analysis-2/ (Accessed 20 August 2021).

edrawmax.com. 2021 'Amazon PESTEL Analysis', Wondershare EdrawMax, [online]. Available at:
https://www.edrawmax.com/article/amazon-pestel-analysis.html (Accessed 20 August 2021).

Editorial Staff. 'Amazon (company)', WIKIPEDIA, [online]. Available at:
https://en.wikipedia.org/wiki/Amazon_(company) (Accessed 20 August 2021).

Editorial Staff. 'AMAZON'S VALUE CHAIN ANALYSIS', BUSINESS STRATEGY INSIGHTS, [online]. Available at:
https://www.bstrategyinsights.com/amazon-value-chain-analysis/ (Accessed 20 August 2021).

Bahadir K., 'Analyzing Starbucks' Value Chain', researchgate, [online]. Available at:
https://www.researchgate.net/figure/Amazoncom-Value-Chain-Analysis-In-technology-stream-has-important-role-to-drive-and_fig3_326132044 (Accessed 12 August 2021).

Taylor B., 2018. 'Value Chain Analysis Of Amazon Com Inc', essay48, [online]. Available at:
https://www.essay48.com/value-chain-analysis/4770-Amazon-com-Inc-Value-Chain-Analysis (Accessed 12 August 2021).
[viii] Amazon.com Inc.'s Generic Strategy, Intensive Growth Strategies http://panmore.com/amazon-com-inc-generic-strategy-intensive-growth-strategies

YOUR KNOWLEDGE HAS VALUE

- We will publish your bachelor's and
  master's thesis, essays and papers

- Your own eBook and book -
  sold worldwide in all relevant shops

- Earn money with each sale

Upload your text at www.GRIN.com
and publish for free

Milton Keynes UK
Ingram Content Group UK Ltd.
UKHW011034201123
432908UK00005BA/774